T0084221

WYDANIE NARODOWE
DZIEŁ FRYDERYKA CHOPINA

NATIONAL EDITION
OF THE WORKS OF FRYDERYK CHOPIN

IMPROMPTUS
Opp. 29, 36, 51

NATIONAL EDITION
Edited by JAN EKIER

Foundation
for the National Edition
of the Works of Fryderyk Chopin

PWM
EDITION

SERIES A. WORKS PUBLISHED DURING CHOPIN'S LIFETIME. VOLUME III

FRYDERYK CHOPIN

IMPROMPTUS
Op. 29, 36, 51

WYDANIE NARODOWE
Redaktor naczelny: JAN EKIER

FUNDACJA WYDANIA NARODOWEGO
POLSKIE WYDAWNICTWO MUZYCZNE SA
WARSZAWA 2023

SERIA A. UTWORY WYDANE ZA ŻYCIA CHOPINA. TOM III

Redakcja tomu: Jan Ekier, Paweł Kamiński

Do każdego tomu dołączone są w formie luźnej wkładki *Komentarz wykonawczy*
i Komentarz źródłowy (skrócony).

Pełne *Komentarze źródłowe* do poszczególnych tomów będą publikowane oddzielnie.

Wydany w oddzielnym tomie *Wstęp do Wydania Narodowego Dzieł Fryderyka Chopina*
– 1. *Zagadnienia edytorskie* obejmuje całokształt ogólnych problemów wydawniczych,
zaś *Wstęp… –* 2. *Zagadnienia wykonawcze –* całokształt ogólnych problemów interpretacyjnych.

Wydane pośmiertnie *Impromptu cis-moll* znajduje się w tomie *Różne utwory* (29 B V)

Editors of this Volume: Jan Ekier, Paweł Kamiński

A *Performance Commentary* and a *Source Commentary (abridged)*
are included in each volume in the form of a loose insert.

Full *Source Commentaries* on each volume will be published separately.

The Introduction to the National Edition of the Works of Fryderyk Chopin
1. *Editorial Problems*, published as a separate volume, covers general matters concerning the publication.
The Introduction… 2. *Performance Issues* covers all general questions of interpretation.

Impromptu in C sharp minor published posthumously is to be found in the volume *Various Compositions* (29 B V)

Impromptu As-dur op. 29 / in A♭ major Op. 29

Impromptu Fis-dur op. 36 / in F♯ major Op. 36

Impromptu Ges-dur op. 51 / in G♭ major Op. 51

about the Impromptus ...

Op. 29

*'I, the undersigned, residing in Paris in 34 rue St. Lazare, confirm that I sold to Messrs. Breitkopf and Härtel
in Leipzig the rights to the below listed works of my composition, namely:*
                      [...]
            Op. 29. Impromptu
                    [...]
*I declare that I ceded the rights to the above mentioned gentlemen without any reservation or restriction, for ever
and for all countries with the exception of France and England, and confirm that I received the arranged fees
for which a separate receipt has been given.*
                                      F. Chopin.'

From a letter sent by Chopin to the company Breitkopf & Härtel in Leipzig, Paris 16 December 1843.

Op. 36

*'I have my manuscripts in order, well noted down. With your polonaises there are six – discounting the 7th Impromptu,
which may be p o o r : I do not yet know myself, as it is too fresh.'*

*'Please read, and immediately send that fool a letter. [...] That wretched Wessel, I shall no longer send him,
that Agréments au Salon, anything ever. Perhaps you do not know that this is how he called my second Impromptu
or one of the Waltzes.'*

From letters sent by F. Chopin to Julian Fontana in Paris, Nohant, 8 October 1839 and 18 September 1841.

Op. 51

*'Besides this, I have composed an Impromptu, several pages in length, but I shall not even propose it, as I wish
to oblige an old acquaintance of mine who for two years has been requesting me earnestly for something
for Mr Hofmeister. I tell you of this, so that you may be aware of my intentions in this matter.'*

From a letter sent by Chopin to the company Breitkopf & Härtel in Leipzig, Paris, 15 December 1842.

*'Dear Friend,
In the Impromptu which you published with the "Gazette" of 9th July, there is a n e r r o r i n p a g e n u m b e r i n g ,
which renders my composition incomprehensible. Far from having the solicitude which our friend Moscheles
brings to his works, I nonetheless on this occasion feel obliged with regard to your subscribers to ask you
to place an e r r a t u m in your next number:*
           p. 3 – read p. 5
           p. 5 – read p. 3.
*Should you be too busy or too lazy to write to me, please limit your reply to this e r r a t u m in the "Gazette",
from which I shall infer that you, Mrs Schlesinger and your children are all keeping well.*
           Yours ever
                    Chopin'

Letter sent by Chopin to Maurice Schlesinger in Paris, Nohant, 22 July 1843.

o Impromptus ...

op. 29

„Ja, niżej podpisany, zamieszkały w Paryżu przy ul. St. Lazare nr 34, potwierdzam, że sprzedałem Panom Breitkopfowi i Härtlowi w Lipsku prawo własności niżej wymienionych utworów mojej kompozycji, a mianowicie:
[...]
op. 29. Impromptu
[...]
Oświadczam, że odstąpiłem prawo własności wymienionym Panom bez żadnego zastrzeżenia ani ograniczenia, po wszystkie czasy i na wszystkie kraje z wyjątkiem Francji i Anglii, i potwierdzam odbiór umówionych honorariów, na które zostało wystawione osobne pokwitowanie.
F. Chopin."

Z listu F. Chopina do firmy Breitkopf i Härtel w Lipsku, Paryż 16 XII 1843.

op. 36

„Mam moje manuskrypta w porządku, dobrze nanotowane. Jest ich sześć z twoimi polonezami – nie rachując 7-go Impromptu, które może kiepskie: jeszcze sam nie wiem, bo za świeże."

„Proszę Cię, przeczytaj i temu durniowi poślij natychmiast list. [...] Szelma Wessel, już mu, temu Agréments au Salon, nic nie poślę nigdy. Może nie wiesz, że moje Impromptu drugie czy któregoś Walca tak przezwał."

Z listów F. Chopina do Juliana Fontany w Paryżu, Nohant, 8 X 1839 i 18 IX 1841.

op. 51

„Poza tym skomponowałem kilkustronicowe Impromptu, ale go nawet nie proponuję, pragnąc zrobić grzeczność jednemu z mych dawnych znajomych, który od dwóch lat usilnie mnie prosi o coś dla p. Hofmeistra. Mówię Panom o tym, aby Panowie znali moje zamiary w tej sprawie."

Z listu F. Chopina do firmy Breitkopf i Härtel w Lipsku, Paryż 15 XII 1842.

„Drogi Przyjacielu,
w Impromptu, które Pan wydał przy «Gazette» z dnia 9 lipca, popełniono błąd w paginacji, co czyni moją kompozycję niezrozumiałą. Daleki od troskliwości, którą otacza swe prace nasz przyjaciel Moscheles, poczytuję sobie jednak tym razem za obowiązek wobec Pana abonentów prosić Go o zamieszczenie w najbliższym numerze następującego erratum:
str. 3 – czytaj str. 5
str. 5 – czytaj str. 3.
Jeśli Pan byłby zbyt zajęty lub zbyt leniwy, by do mnie napisać – to proszę mi odpowiedzieć tylko za pomocą tego erratum w «Gazette», co będzie znaczyło dla mnie, że Pan, Pani Schlesinger i Pańskie dzieci jesteście wszyscy zdrowi.
Całkowicie oddany Panu
Chopin."

List F. Chopina do Maurycego Schlesingera w Paryżu, Nohant, 22 VII 1843.

Impromptu
A Mademoiselle Caroline de Lobau

Allegro assai quasi Presto

op. 29

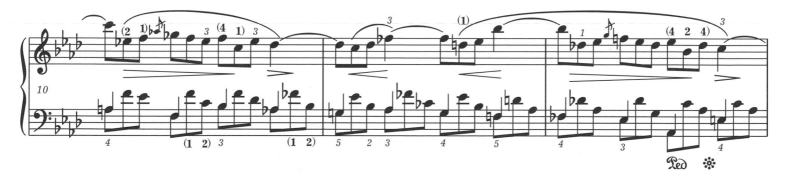

11

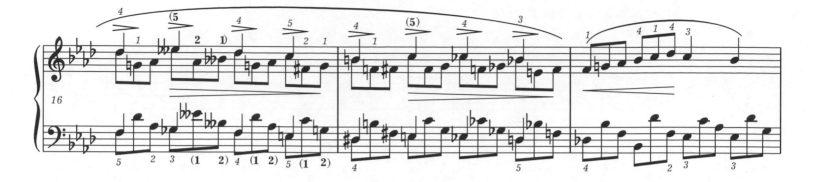

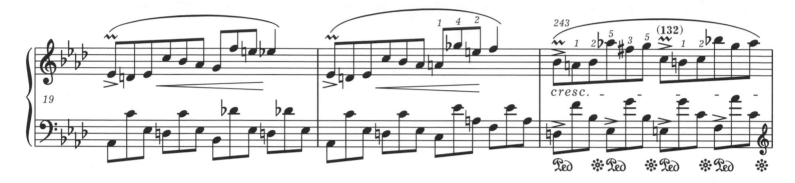

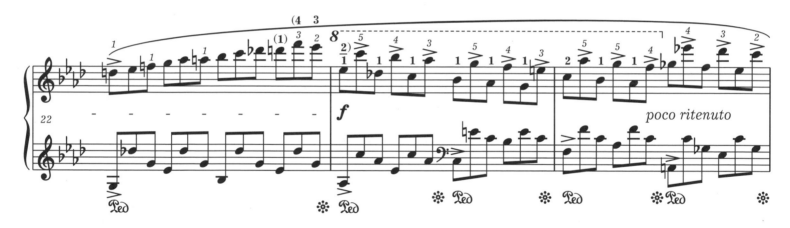

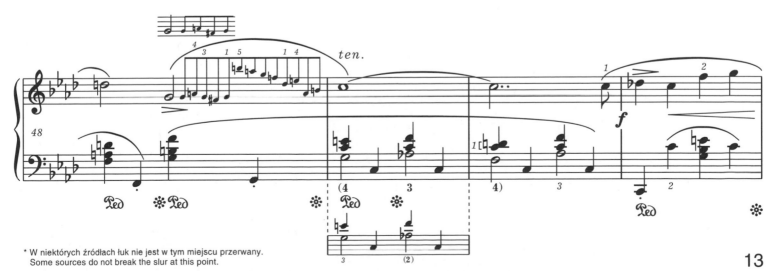

* W niektórych źródłach łuk nie jest w tym miejscu przerwany.
  Some sources do not break the slur at this point.

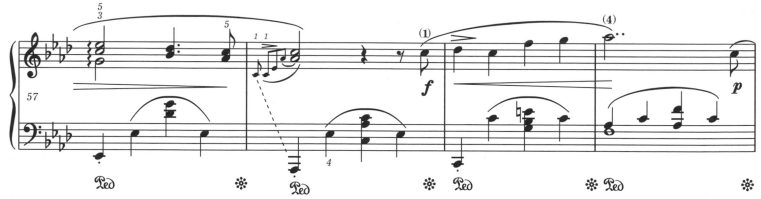

14

ossia:

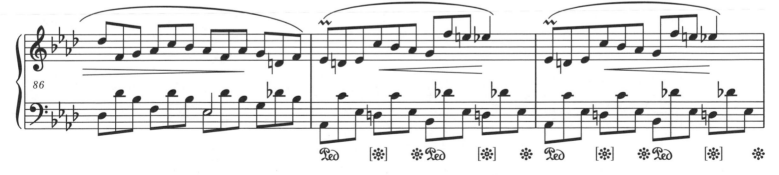

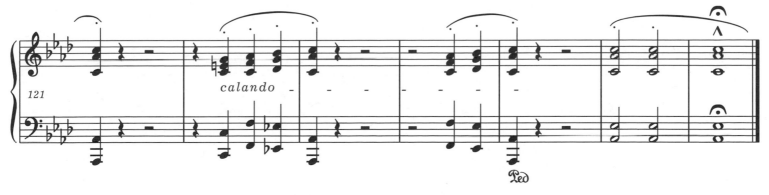

Impromptu

* W jednym ze źródeł **Allegretto**. Patrz *Komentarz źródłowy*.
In one of the sources **Allegretto**. Vide *Source Commentary*.

** Inne autentyczne łukowanie l.r. w t. 28-29:
Different authentic slurring in L.H. in bars 28-29:

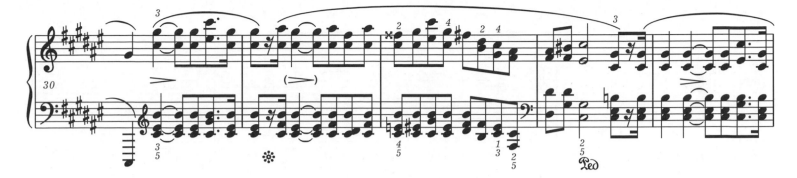

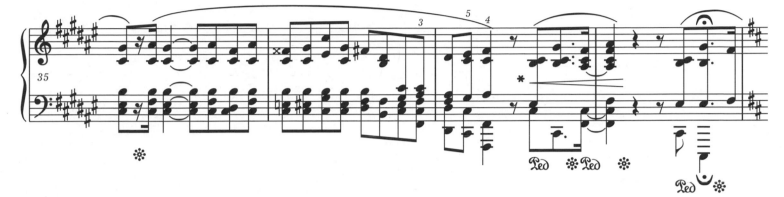

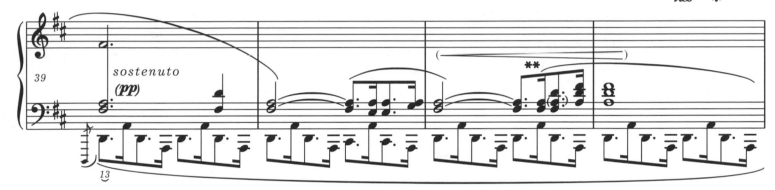

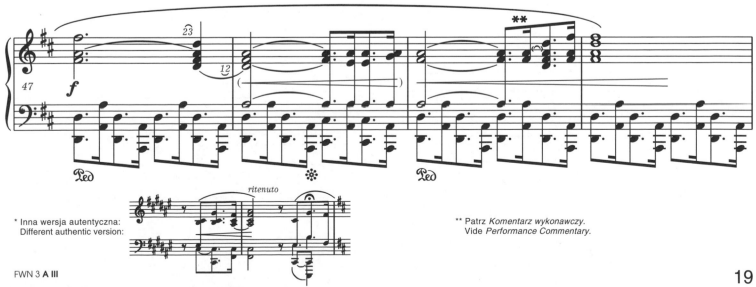

* Inna wersja autentyczna:
   Different authentic version:

** Patrz *Komentarz wykonawczy.*
   Vide *Performance Commentary.*

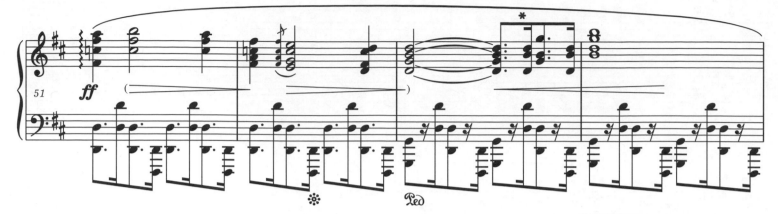

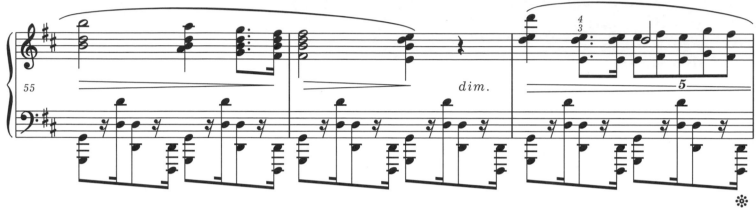

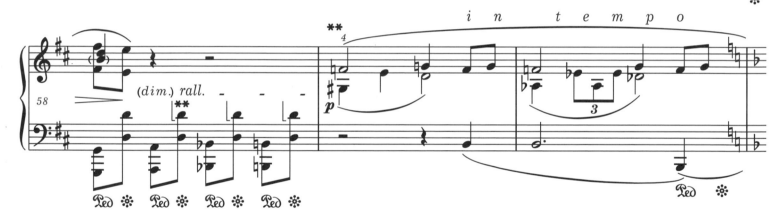

* Autentyczny wariant wykonawczy: . Patrz *Komentarz wykonawczy* do t. 41, 49 i 53.
  Authentic performance variant: . Vide *Performance Commentary* to bars 41, 49 and 53.

** Patrz *Komentarz wykonawczy*.
   Vide *Performance Commentary*.

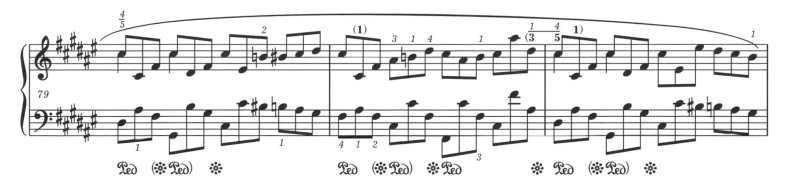

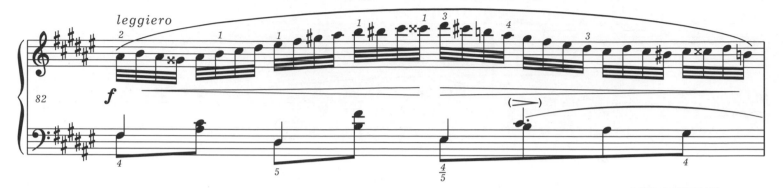

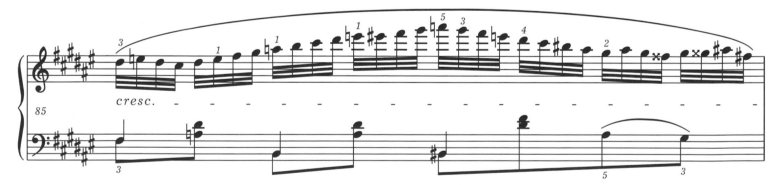

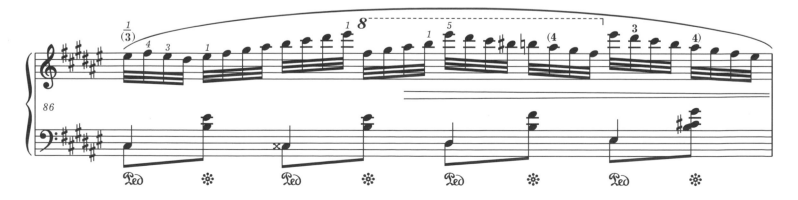

* Warianty w t. 83 i 89 należy traktować łącznie.
  The variants in bars 83 and 89 should be treated jointly.

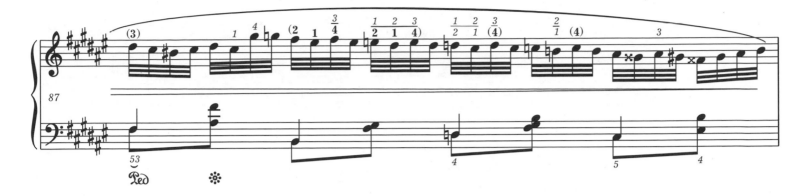

* ossia: *pp*.
** Wariant jak w t. 83.
   Variant as in bar 83.

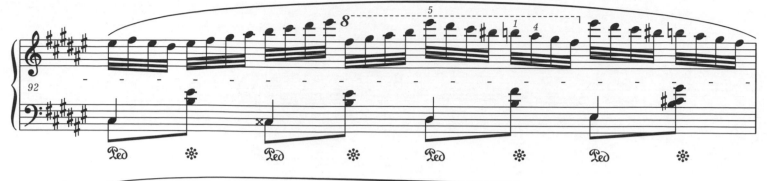

24

* Wariant jak w t. 37-38:
  Variant as in bars 37-38:

Impromptu

A Madame la Comtesse Esterházy née Comtesse Batthyany

op. 51

3

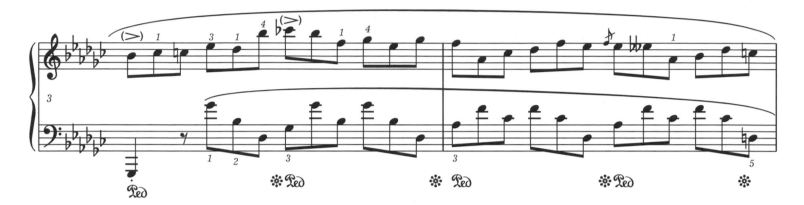

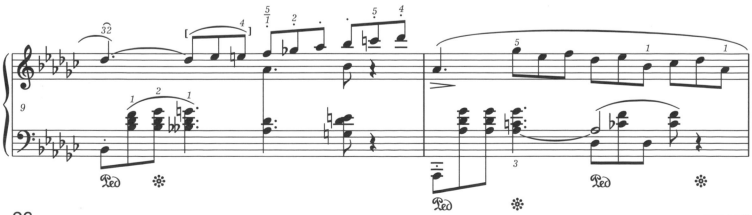

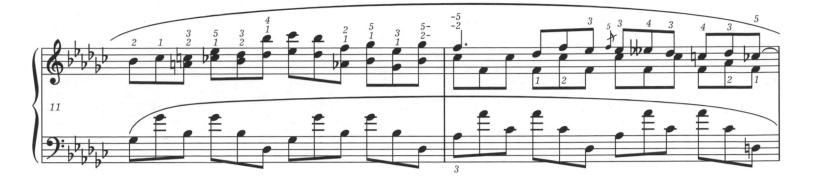

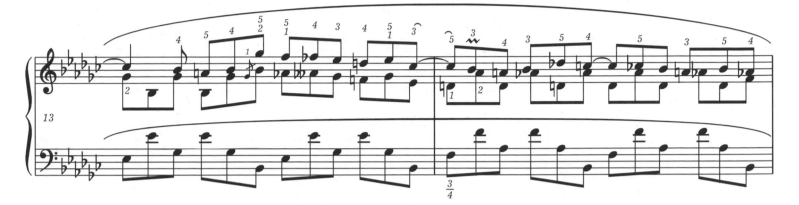

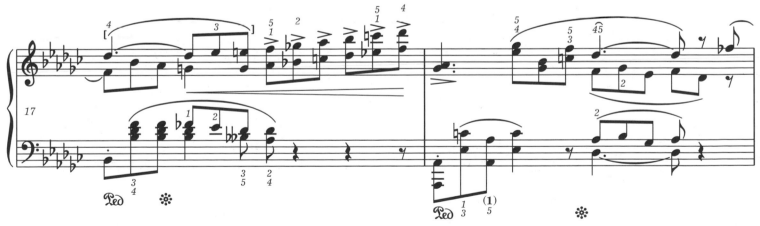

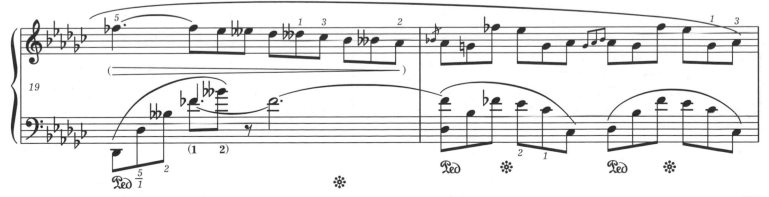

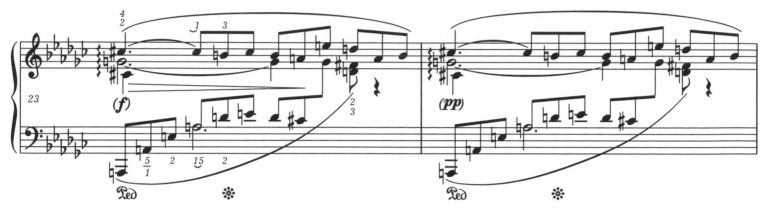

28

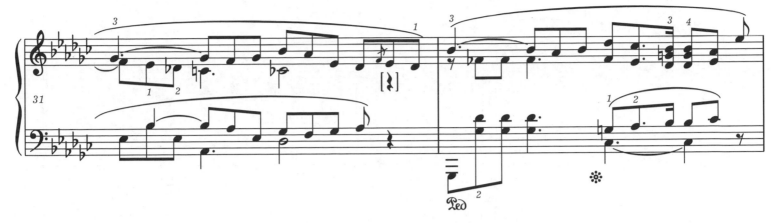

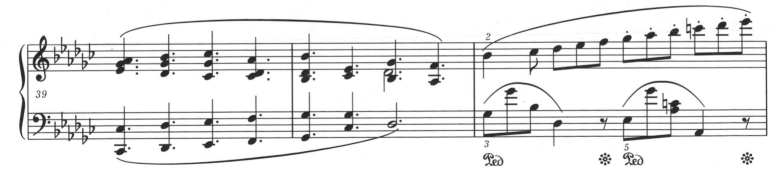

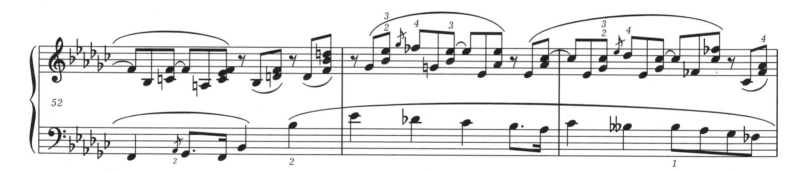

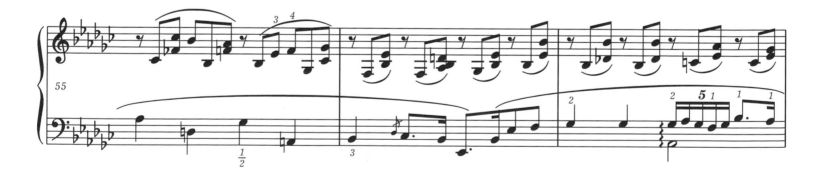

30

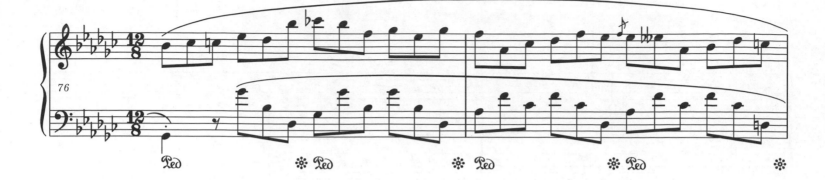

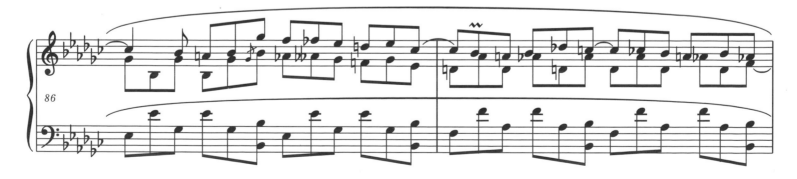

32

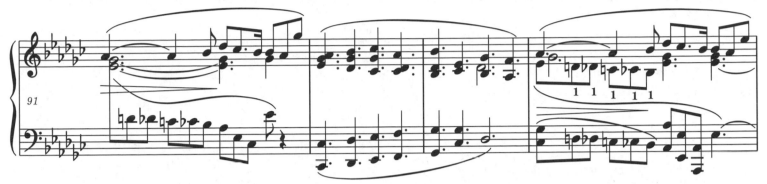

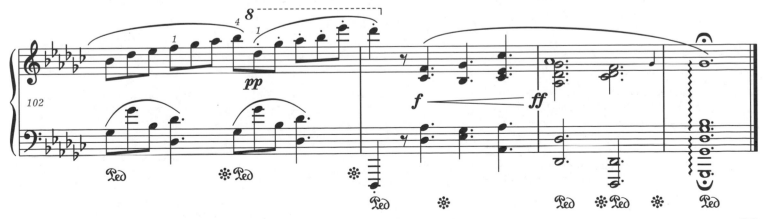

NATIONAL EDITION OF THE WORKS OF FRYDERYK CHOPIN

Plan of the edition

Series A. WORKS PUBLISHED DURING CHOPIN'S LIFETIME

Series B. WORKS PUBLISHED POSTHUMOUSLY

(The titles in square brackets [] have been reconstructed by the National Edition; the titles in slant marks // are still in use today but are definitely, or very probably, not authentic)

1 **A I**   **Ballades** Opp. 23, 38, 47, 52

2 **A II**   **Etudes** Opp. 10, 25, Three Etudes (Méthode des Méthodes)

3 **A III**   **Impromptus** Opp. 29, 36, 51

4 **A IV**   **Mazurkas (A)** Opp. 6, 7, 17, 24, 30, 33, 41, Mazurka in a (Gaillard), Mazurka in a (from the album La France Musicale /Notre Temps/), Opp. 50, 56, 59, 63   25 **B I**   **Mazurkas (B)** in B♭, G, a, C, F, G, B♭, A♭, C, a, g, f

5 **A V**   **Nocturnes** Opp. 9, 15, 27, 32, 37, 48, 55, 62

6 **A VI**   **Polonaises (A)** Opp. 26, 40, 44, 53, 61   26 **B II**   **Polonaises (B)** in B♭, g, A♭, g♯, d, f, b♭, B♭, G♭

7 **A VII** **Preludes** Opp. 28, 45

8 **A VIII** **Rondos** Opp. 1, 5, 16

9 **A IX** **Scherzos** Opp. 20, 31, 39, 54

10 **A X**   **Sonatas** Opp. 35, 58

11 **A XI**   **Waltzes (A)** Opp. 18, 34, 42, 64   27 **B III**   **Waltzes (B)** in E, b, D♭, A♭, e, G♭, A♭, f, a

12 **A XII** **Various Works (A)** Variations brillantes Op. 12, Bolero, Tarantella, Allegro de concert, Fantaisie Op. 49, Berceuse, Barcarolle; *supplement* – Variation VI from "Hexameron"   28 **B IV**   **Various Works (B)** Variations in E, Sonata in c (Op. 4)

29 **B V**   **Various Compositions** Funeral March in c, [Variants] /Souvenir de Paganini/, Nocturne in e, Ecossaises in D, G, D♭, Contredanse, [Allegretto], Lento con gran espressione /Nocturne in c♯/, Cantabile in B♭, Presto con leggierezza /Prelude in A♭/, Impromptu in c♯ /Fantaisie-Impromptu/, "Spring" (version for piano), Sostenuto /Waltz in E♭/, Moderato /Feuille d'Album/, Galop Marquis, Nocturne in c

13 **A XIIIa** **Concerto in E minor** Op. 11 for piano and orchestra (version for one piano)   30 **B VIa** **Concerto in E minor** Op. 11 for piano and orchestra (version with second piano)

14 **A XIIIb** **Concerto in F minor** Op. 21 for piano and orchestra (version for one piano)   31 **B VIb** **Concerto in F minor** Op. 21 for piano and orchestra (version with second piano)

15 **A XIVa** **Concert Works** for piano and orchestra Opp. 2, 13, 14 (version for one piano)   32 **B VII** **Concert Works** for piano and orchestra Opp. 2, 13, 14, 22 (version with second piano)

16 **A XIVb** **Grande Polonaise in E♭ major** Op. 22 for piano and orchestra (version for one piano)

17 **A XVa** **Variations on "Là ci darem" from "Don Giovanni"** Op. 2. Score

18 **A XVb** **Concerto in E minor** Op. 11. Score (historical version)   33 **B VIIIa** **Concerto in E minor** Op. 11. Score (concert version)

19 **A XVc** **Fantasia on Polish Airs** Op. 13. Score

20 **A XVd** **Krakowiak** Op. 14. Score

21 **A XVe** **Concerto in F minor** Op. 21. Score (historical version)   34 **B VIIIb** **Concerto in F minor** Op. 21. Score (concert version)

22 **A XVf** **Grande Polonaise in E♭ major** Op. 22. Score

23 **A XVI** **Works for Piano and Cello** Polonaise Op. 3, Grand Duo Concertant, Sonata Op. 65   35 **B IX**   **Rondo in C** for two pianos; **Variations in D** for four hands; *addendum* – working version of Rondo in C (for one piano)

24 **A XVII** **Piano Trio** Op. 8   36 **B X**   **Songs**

37 **Supplement** Compositions partly by Chopin: Hexameron, Mazurkas in F♯, D, D, C, Variations for Flute and Piano; harmonizations of songs and dances: "The Dąbrowski Mazurka", "God who hast embraced Poland" (Largo) Bourrées in G, A, Allegretto in A-major/minor

FRYDERYK CHOPIN
IMPROMPTUS

Performance Commentary
Source Commentary (abridged)

PERFORMANCE COMMENTARY

Notes on the musical text

The v a r i a n t s marked *ossia* were indicated as such by Chopin himself, or added in his handwriting to pupils' copies; the variants without this designation are the result of discrepancies in the authentic sources or the impossibility of arriving at an unambiguous reading of the text.

Minor authentic alternatives (individual notes, ornaments, slurs, accents, pedal markings, etc.), that can be considered variants, are enclosed in parentheses. Editorial additions are enclosed in brackets.

Pianists not interested in source-related questions, who wish to base their performance on a single text without variants, are advised to use the music printed on the principle staves, including all the markings in parentheses or brackets.

Chopin's original f i n g e r i n g is indicated in large bold-type numerals (**1 2 3 4 5**), in contrast to the editors' fingering, written in smaller italic numerals (*1 2 3 4 5*). Original fingering enclosed in parentheses indicates fingering not present in the primary sources, but added by Chopin to his pupils' copies.

A general discussion of the interpretation of Chopin's works will be contained in a separate volume, *Introduction to the National Edition,* in the section entitled *Problems of Performance.*

Abbreviations: R.H. – right hand, L.H. – left hand.

Impromptu in A flat major, Op. 29

p. 11 *Bar 1 and similar.* R.H. Beginning the mordent simultaneously with the first note of the L.H. should be deemed more correct than anticipated execution (the third note of the mordent together with the bass note). In any case, most important is the singing and rhythmically smooth leading of the melody line created by the accented principal note of the mordent and the further quavers of the R.H.

The *legato* probably applies also to the L.H., and may refer to 'harmonic legato' (the fingers sustain components of the harmony):

In opting for this type of execution, one must ensure that the held notes, supplementing, as it were, the pedalling, do not burden the accompaniment.

p. 13 *Bar 41* R.H. In the editors' opinion, the most adroit rhythmic resolution of the appoggiatura is as follows:

In this context (within the slur) the dot above the *db²* may indicate a momentary suspension of the *legato* articulation, the continuity of the longer phrase idea being maintained.

Bar 45 R.H. A sense of calm and ease is imparted by a realisation of the group of small notes similar to the following:

p. 14 *Bars 62-63 and 78-79* The beginning of the trills preceded by grace notes in bars 62 and 78:

The first notes of the R.H., *g²* in bar 62 and *a²* in bar 78, should be struck simultaneously to the top note of the L.H. arpeggio, *gb¹*. The other arpeggios of the L.H. should also be executed in an anticipated manner, with their top note, *f¹*, falling on the first note of the successive trills in the R.H., *bb²* and *b²*.

p. 15 *Bar 81* R.H. Alternative fingering:

p. 17 *Bars 117-118* The execution of these two bars on a single pedal, as prescribed by Chopin, may sound too dense on modern pianos with the pedal pressed down fully. In order to obtain the effect of the gentle blending of harmonic functions intended by the composer, the editors recommend the use of a 'half-pedal' (light pressing down of the pedal so as to muffle the shorter and more lightly struck strings, and to preserve the sound of the bass ground and of the accented notes in the treble).

Impromptu in F sharp major, Op. 36

p. 18 *Bars 1, 2 and similar.* L.H. Should a performer's limited L.H. span require the use of an arpeggio in executing the ninth, it would be better to play the upper note with the R.H., so that the notes still sound together.

Bars 29-30 On modern pianos, applying Chopin's pedalling to preserve the beautiful harmonic background for the subsequent phrase creates the risk of an overly intense resonance of the clash *b¹-a#¹-g#¹*. This can be avoided by means of the following device:

p. 19 *Bars 41, 49 and 53* R.H. The variants in these bars should be treated integrally, since the sources indicate two somewhat divergent pianistic conceptions of these places (cf. *Source Commentary*):

	1)	2)
bars 41-42		
bars 49-50		
bars 53-54		

In the former, the greater quantity of struck (repeated) notes impels one to a firmer articulation; in the latter, the holding or skipping of notes allows for a more precise legato in the upper part and a calmer hand position.

Bars 47-57 The convergence of the parts of the two hands in bars 48-49 and 52-53 affords the possibility of the first finger of the R.H. taking over some of the upper notes of the L.H. octaves, which facilitates the L.H. leaps. This combination can also be applied in the remaining bars of this section.

p. 20 *Bar 57* In the second half of the bar, attention should be brought to the smooth rhythm and sound of the R.H. quintuplet, fitting to this the rhythm of the L.H. The synchronisation of the two hands can be considerably facilitated by striking the third of the five R.H. octaves simultaneously with the second (semiquaver) octave of the L.H.:

The lapse of time theoretically occurring between these two strokes is so short that in practice the specified execution is indistinguishable from a strict rhythmic realisation.

Bar 58 Vertical lines added to the notes d^1 in the pupils' copies most probably indicate that these notes, or possibly the whole octaves d-d^1, should be played with the R.H. It is also possible to extend the notes played by the R.H. to the value of a crotchet.

Bars 59-60 It is not clear from the sources (cf. *Source Commentary*) how Chopin imagined the return to the main tempo, which is unquestionable at the beginning of bar 61. The editors suggest the following execution: after slowing down in bar 58, bar 59 should be commenced somewhat below the basic tempo, and the music subsequently animated so as to return to the proper (initial) tempo at the beginning of bar 61.

p. 21 *Bars 75-78* R.H. Woven into the triplet figuration is the continuation of the theme begun in bar 73. In Chopin's notation, some of the hidden thematic notes are indicated with additional stems, the value of a minim, or placement on the upper staff. The method of combining these elements in a cohesive phrase and its presentation to the listener – through the delicate emphasising of appropriate notes – is left to the artistic taste and pianistic abilities of the performer.

p. 22 *Bars 82-93* The signs f and p appearing in bars 82 and 88 should be read more as indicating a differentiation in expression rather than merely in dynamics (for there is *leggiero* in force). Other dynamic markings also should not be too greatly emphasised (they occur in some of the sources only, cf. *Source Commentary*).

Impromptu in G flat major, Op. 51

p. 30 *Bars 49-69* L.H. ♩. ♪ = ♪ ³ ♪ . Cf. *Source Commentary*.

p. 31 *Bars 74-75* The *ritenuto* does not suggest a precise fragment of deceleration. If needs be, the return to tempo, unquestionable at the beginning of bar 76, can be subtly anticipated in the second half of bar 75.

p. 33 *Bar 105* The arpeggios should be executed in a continuous manner (gb in the R.H. after db in the L.H.).

Jan Ekier
Paweł Kamiński

SOURCE COMMENTARY (ABRIDGED)

Initial remarks

The present commentary sets out in abridged form the principles be-
hind the editing of the musical text of each particular work and dis-
cusses the more important discrepancies between authentic sources; in
addition, it signals the most common departures from the authentic text
encountered in the collected editions of Chopin's works prepared after
the composer's death. A precise characterisation of the sources, their
relations to one another, the justification of the choice of basic sources,
a detailed presentation of the differences appearing between them, and
also reproductions of characteristic fragments of the different sources
are all contained in a separately published *Source Commentary*.

Abbreviations: R.H. – right hand; L.H. – left hand. The sign → indicates a rela-
tionship between sources, and should be read as 'and the source based thereon'.

Note to the second edition

In working on the present edition of the *Impromptus*, use was made of
several sources not taken into consideration during the preparation of
the first edition (PWM, Cracow 1983), which enabled the editors to be
more precise with regard to the solutions put forward and more scru-
pulous in the choice of variants.

Impromptu in A flat major, Op. 29

Sources
A   Autograph fair copy intended as the basis for the original German
    edition (Fryderyk Chopin Museum, Warsaw). More than ten acci-
    dentals added in pencil are most probably the work of the en-
    graver of this edition. The notation of **A** displays numerous omis-
    sions of accidentals, and in the final section of the work (from
    bar 83) also a range of other inaccuracies (cf. notes to bars 83-
    90, 87-94, 93 and 121).
GE1 Original German edition, Breitkopf & Härtel (5850), Leipzig, Novem-
    ber 1837, based on **A**. In **GE**1 most of the missing accidentals were
    added, and those erroneously added in **A** amended. Chopin may
    have contributed to these corrections. There are copies of **GE**1
    differing in price or in the graphic layout of the cover (three types).
GE2 Second German edition (same publisher and plate number),
    c. 1853. The accidentals are amended here, and several arbit-
    rary changes are made (the most important in bar 11).
GE3 Second, revised impression of **GE**2, c. 1866.
GE4 Third impression of **GE**2, with an altered version of bars 11
    and 93. There are copies of **GE**4 differing in the cover price.
GE = **GE**1, **GE**2, **GE**3 and **GE**4.
FE Original French edition, M. Schlésinger (M.S. 1499), Paris, Octo-
    ber 1837. **FE** is based on a lost manuscript (autograph or copy)
    and may have been corrected by Chopin.
FED, FES, FEJ – pupils' copies of **FE** with Chopin's additions of fin-
    gering and corrections of printing errors:
    FED – copy from the collection belonging to Chopin's pupil Camille
    Dubois (Bibliothèque Nationale, Paris); also contains a variant
    and several performance markings.
    FES – copy from the collection belonging to Chopin's pupil Jane
    Stirling (Bibliothèque Nationale, Paris).
    FEJ – copy from the collection belonging to Chopin's sister Lud-
    wika Jędrzejewiczowa (Fryderyk Chopin Museum, Warsaw).
EE1 First English edition, Wessel & C° (W & C° 2166), London, Octo-
    ber 1837, based on a lost manuscript (other than **FE**). **EE** bears
    traces of editorial alterations, and was most probably not cor-
    rected by Chopin. There are copies of **EE**1 with different covers.
EE2 Later impression of **EE**1 (from 1848-1851), in which several
    errors and inaccuracies have been amended.
EE = **EE**1 and **EE**2.

The relationships and chronology of the sources are not
clear in the case of this *Impromptu*. Each of the original editions is
most probably based on a different manuscript, yet it is difficult to say
whether **FE** and **EE** were based on copies of **A** or – as a range of evidence suggests – on an earlier autograph and its copy (now lost). What-
ever the case may be, Chopin probably carried out final adjustments to
all three already completed manuscripts. Meanwhile, there is no clear
evidence of his contribution to the proofreading of editions, although
this is not impossible, particularly in the case of **FE** and **GE**.

Editorial principles
We adopt **A** as the basic source, compared with **FE** and **EE**. We take
into account Chopin's additions to the pupils' copies. The relatively
numerous – especially in **A** and **FE** – omissions of accidentals are
amended without comment.
All three pupils' copies contain abundant Chopin fingering. For
practical reasons, figures indicated by the composer in the recapitulation only (in bars 83-114) are shifted in the present edition to corresponding bars in the first section.

p. 11   *Bar 1* **FE** and **GE** have the time signature **c**. This is most prob-
    ably an inaccuracy encountered on many occasions in Chopin
    works published by these companies (cf. e.g. commentary to
    the *Etude in C* Op. 10 No. 1, bar 1).

    Bars 7 and 89 R.H. Above the first note $\sim\!\sim$ is missing in **FE**.
    This is most probably an oversight.

    Bars 10 and 92 L.H. As the third quaver **A** (→**GE**) and **FE** have eb^1,
    whereas **EE** has c^1. Corrections in bar 10 of **A** prove that after in-
    itial hesitation over this note Chopin eventually decided on eb^1.

    Bar 11 R.H. In **GE**2 the second and third quavers were changed
    arbitrarily to d^2 and eb^2. The correct version was restored in **GE**4.
    Cf. note to bar 93.

p. 12   *Bars 21 and 103* R.H. Missing above the first note in **FE** is $\sim\!\sim$.
    In bar 21 Chopin corrected this error in **FE**S and **FE**J.

    Bars 22-24 and 104-106 L.H. In **FE** there are no accents (apart
    from the accent on the *c* in bar 105). This is most probably an
    oversight by the engraver or copyist.

    Bar 24 Added at the beginning of the bar in **FE**D (most probably
    by the hand of the pupil) is the marking *rit.*

p. 13   *Bar 38* L.H. As the third crotchet **FE** erroneously has the chord
    g-bb-db^1-f^1, which Chopin corrected in all the pupils' copies.

    Bar 40 L.H. At the beginning of the bar some later collected
    editions arbitrarily added a c^1 to the sixth g-eb^1.
    R.H. In **A** Chopin changed the slurring in this bar. It would ap-
    pear more likely that the continuous slur initially written was sub-
    sequently divided; in the present edition such slurs are repro-
    duced in the main text (such is also the case in **EE**). It is possi-
    ble, however, that in **A** Chopin joined the slurs (**FE** has a con-
    tinuous slur). In **GE** a new slur begins from the first note of this
    bar (a misreading of **A**).

    Bar 41 R.H. The dot above the db^2 is found only in **A** (→**GE**).
    Cf. *Performance Commentary*.

    Bar 48 R.H. The main text is reproduced from **A**. Initially, the turn
    in the second half of the bar began with the second note, a^1. Cho-
    pin subsequently added the small note g^1 in such a way that it
    touches the preceding minim g^1. One may consider whether this
    indicates the convergence of the voices (in which case the note g^1
    would not need repeating). However, such a reading is opposed by
    the following arguments:

– Chopin did not have room in **A** to add a note at the beginning of the run and preserve sufficient distance from the minim g^1;
– the convergence of the voices could have been indicated more clearly and simply by adding another stem to the minim and extending the beam of the run (Chopin employed this kind of notation very often):

The reading of **A** adopted in the present edition appears in **FE** and **GE**. The version from **EE** given as a variant can be considered an alternative correction by Chopin of the original version of the run. A similar tracing of the melodic line can be found e.g. in the *Nocturne in Bb minor* Op. 9 No. 1, bars 3 and 73.

Bar 49 L.H. The main text comes from **A** (→**GE**), the variant from **FE**. In **EE** a triad appears on the first crotchet, and a sixth on the third. The lack of c^1 is highly likely to be due to oversight, although Chopin does appear to have accepted this version in lessons. This is clear from fingering written into two pupils' copies, one of which (the second finger on ab added in **FE**J) precludes the use of a triad.

Bar 50 L.H. Missing before the first chord in **A** (→**GE**1), **FE** and **EE** is the ♮ raising db^1 to d^1. Chopin added this in all three extant pupils' copies. In **GE**2 ♭ has been added arbitrarily, subsequently altered to ♮ in **GE**3. In **EE** the middle note of this chord is erroneously bb.

Bar 59 R.H. In **FE**J added above the second crotchet is the fingering 2. We do not give it, on the assumption that it is inadvertently placed one crotchet too early.

p. 14

Bar 62 R.H. Added arbitrarily in the ending of the trill in most later collected editions is ♯ , raising g^2 to $g\sharp^2$. *See* note to bar 78.

Bar 64 L.H. **A** (→**GE**1→**GE**2), **FE** and **EE** have c^2 and ab^1 as the third and fourth crotchets. Chopin corrected his error in **FE**J. **GE**3 (→**GE**4) also has the correct version.

Bar 71 R.H. As the penultimate note of the bar, **EE** has $f\sharp^1$. Given that before the tenth and twelfth notes **A**, **FE** and **EE**1 lack the accidentals restoring the f^2 and eb^2, it seems likely that this ♯ was added by the reviser of **EE**1, misled by the ♯ still in force before the tenth note of the bar ($f\sharp^2$). Meanwhile, appropriate corrections, involving the addition of the omitted signs, were made in **GE**1 (♮ f^2) and **GE**2 (♭ eb^2), and also in **EE**2 (both signs), although this source does retain the aforementioned redundant ♯ before the fourteenth note.

p. 15

Bar 74 R.H. In **A** the minim stem reaches down only to the top note of the chord (c^2). Thus, the three remaining notes can be seen as semibreves , which from a formal point of view is a strict notation. However, Chopin did not always scrupulously extend the stem to all the notes of the chord, thus the notation of **A** may also be understood as . Since, providing the correct pedalling is employed, the two notations give the same sound, we adopt this second interpretation as closer to a practical execution. In **FE** all the elements of the chord have the value of a dotted minim, and in **EE** of a double-dotted minim; both notations were probably amended without the participation of Chopin. **GE** has the notation adopted by us.

Bars 75-76 The pedalling is to be found only in **EE**.

Bar 77 R.H. In **FE** the crotchet stems are missing from d^2 and g^2.

Bar 78 R.H. The grace note a^2, indicating the beginning of the trill from the principal note, comes from **A** (→**GE**) and **EE**. In **FE** the grace note takes the form of a small crotchet g^2. This is most probably an error, as is indicated by the following circumstances:

— the lack of ♮ before the trilled minim a^2; the sign is not necessary when the note is preceded by a grace note of the same pitch;
— the beginning of a trill from a lower second was generally shown by Chopin by means of a double grace note (as he did in bar 62);
— given the different melodic shaping of the ending of the preceding phrase, Chopin probably deliberately differentiated between the trills in bars 62 and 78.
The lack of a clear correction of the pitch of the grace note in the pupils' copies does not necessarily testify to Chopin's acceptance of the version with the grace note g^2:
— in **FE**S ♮ is added before the minim in such a way that it may also indicate the modification of the pitch of the grace note;
— **FE**D and **FE**J have no annotation here.

Bar 81 L.H. In **FE**D Chopin added 8^a beneath the chord. As an *ossia* variant, we give the most probable reading of this addition, notated in a manner Chopin employed in analogous situations, e.g. in the *Etude in Gb* Op. 10 No. 5, bar 65.

Bars 83-90 and 103-104 **A** (→**GE**) has no pedal marks here. As this is most probably an oversight by Chopin (cf. note to bars 87-94), we give the marking of **FE**. It is difficult to assess whether the pedalling in bars 83-84 and 87-88 (longer, half-bar pedals), which is somewhat divergent from that of similar bars, is an authentic execution variant or is merely due to imprecise notation. The asterisks ✻ in parentheses in bars 83-84 come from **EE**, which gives pedalling only in bars 83-85 and 103-104.

Bars 87-94 In **A** (→**GE**) the only dynamic mark is ⤙ in bar 89. Given that both previously and subsequently the markings appearing in **A** are analogous to those of the first section of the work, this omission is most probably of an accidental nature. Thus we reproduce the markings of **FE**, in accordance with the markings appearing in all sources in bars 5-12. Similar markings also occur in **EE**, with the exception of marks omitted in bar 93.

p. 16

Bar 93 R.H. The main text comes from **FE** and **EE**, while the version given in the footnote comes from **A** (→**GE**, except **GE**4, which uses the text of **FE** and **EE**). We give priority to the version in keeping with the corresponding bar of the opening section of the *Impromptu* (bar 11), taking into account the following arguments:
— the melody in the main version (c^2-db^2) evolves more coherently and naturally – all the ascending motifs appearing in bars 91-95 after the crotchet interruption of the triplet movement begin with a note lower than the preceding one;
— it is possible that the version with d^2-eb^2, in which the melodic shaping appearing two bars earlier is repeated exactly, is the original version of bars 11 and 93, corrected by Chopin in lost manuscripts (e.g. in the bases for **FE** and **EE**); the change to c^2-db^2 would be an audible enrichment of the melodic line;
— there are no other significant differences between the outermost sections of the work (bars 1-30 and 83-112); moreover, it is entirely likely that in the manuscripts forming the basis for **FE** and **EE** bars 83-112 were marked in abridged form only, as a repetition of bars 1-30 (cf. notes to bars 7, 10, 21 and 105-107);
— in writing **A**, Chopin notated bars 83-112 less carefully than their corresponding bars 1-30, as is testified to, *inter alia*, by the incomplete and inconsistent pedalling and dynamics (cf. notes to bars 83-90 and 87-94); thus, in the bar in question the exact repetition of the melodic shape of bar 91 may have been written out inadvertently (such a momentary lapse of concentration affected Chopin in bar 96, where one sees the deletion of the first triplet of the L.H., inadvertently repeated after bar 95; see also note to bar 121); this kind of slip becomes even more likely if the version with d^2-eb^2 was the original version.

Bars 103 and 106 R.H. The fourth and tenth quavers of bar 103 (ab^2 and bb^2) and the eighth note of bar 106 (eb^3) are preceded in **A** by naturals, most probably added by the engraver of **GE**. These errors were later corrected in the proofs of **GE**1.

Bars 105-107 R.H. **FE** and **EE** repeat here the fingering from bars 23-25.

p. 17

Bars 113-119 **EE** prescribes one pedal from the beginning of bar 113 to the rest after the first chord of bar 115; similarly in bars 117-110. This is most probably the original conception, as testified by the deletion in **A** of the sign 🎵 at the beginning of bar 113 (cf. note to bars 115 and 119). In **FE** there are only short pedals at the beginning of bars 115 and 119. We give the pedalling of **A** (→**GE**), in which bars 113-114 and 117-118 are treated differently (cf. *Performance Commentary*).

Bars 115 and 119 L.H. On the second crotchet of the bar **EE** has the octave *C-c*. This is most probably the original version, as testified by Chopin's deletion of the octave in bar 119 in **A**.
Instead of *sotto voce* **EE** has *p* (and in bar 115 also *legatissimo*). These are probably earlier indications rejected by Chopin, since in **A** the *p* initially written in bar 115 was subsequently changed by Chopin to *sotto voce*. Cf. note to bars 113-119. **FE** has only *sotto voce* in bar 115.

Bar 121 **A** (→**GE**) notes the chord as a quaver followed by a quaver pause (as in bar 117). Such a substantial shortening of the value appears to be unnecessary here, hence our adoption of the more natural notation of **FE** and **EE**. It is possible that Chopin inadvertently transcribed in **A** the version from bar 117 (cf. note to bar 93).

Bars 122-124 **FE** has no *calando*, whilst **EE** has *smorz.* instead of *calando* in bar 124. Cf. note to bars 113-119.

Bars 126-127 **EE** has the following, probably original, notation (*see* note to bars 113-119 and to bars 115 and 119):

The articulation marks for the L.H. are probably editorial additions; similar supplements of markings – with different rhythmic values – were also effected in **GE**.

Impromptu in F sharp major, Op. 36

Sources
AI Fragment (bars 30-38 and from bar 70 to the end) of a working autograph, partially sketched (two pages in the Chopin Society in Warsaw, two in the Cracow National Museum). Bars 82-100 were initially written in double rhythmic values, which Chopin already changed in **AI**. In quite numerous instances of discrepancies between original editions, **AI** allows one to identify the earlier (original) versions.
GE1 Original German edition, Breitkopf & Härtel (6333), Leipzig, May 1840, based on a lost (probably autograph) manuscript. Chopin most probably did not proofread **GE1**. There are copies of **GE1** differing in cover price.
GE2 Second impression of **GE1**, after 1860, in which some of the errors were amended and a few changes made arbitrarily.
GE = **GE1** and **GE2**.
FE1 Original French edition, E. Troupenas et Cie (T. 892), Paris, May 1840, based on another lost manuscript (probably also an autograph). Chopin may possibly have proofread **FE1**.
FE2 Second impression of **FE1**, corrected by Chopin.
FE3 Third impression of **FE1**, corrected most probably with Chopin's participation. This impression was reprinted after Chopin's death by the publishers Brandus et Cie, with the latter's plate number (B. et Cie 6477) added.
FE = **FE1**, **FE2** and **FE3**.

FESch, FES, FED – pupils' copies of **FE** with additions by Chopin containing various performance markings, fingering and corrections of printing errors:
FESch – copy of **FE1** from the collection belonging to Chopin's pupil Marie de Scherbatoff (Houghton Library, New York);
FES – copy of **FE2** from the collection belonging to Chopin's pupil Jane Stirling (Bibliothèque Nationale, Paris);
FED – copy of **FE3** from the collection belonging to Chopin's pupil Camille Dubois (Bibliothèque Nationale, Paris).
EE1 Original English edition, Wessel & C° (W & C° 3550), London, June 1840. **EE1** is probably based on a copy of **FE1** with additions by Chopin and was not itself proofread by him. It bears evidence of editorial alterations.
EE2 Second impression of **EE1**, 1843, in which several errors were amended and the original version restored at the end of bar 92 and the beginning of bar 93.

Editorial principles
Adopted as the basic source is **FE**, as one undoubtedly corrected by Chopin. We take account of improvements probably made by Chopin to the bases of **GE** and **EE**, as well as his annotations to the pupils' copies.
Performance markings in parentheses, unless indicated otherwise further in the commentary, come from **GE**. Minor elements appearing in **GE** (*staccato* dots, pedal marks, the prolonging of certain notes), whose absence from **FE** can be deemed an oversight on the part of Chopin, are given without brackets.

p. 18

Bar 1 **Andantino** appears in **FE** (→**EE**), **Allegretto** in **GE**.
FE (→**EE**) has the time signature **C** instead of **¢**, which appears in **GE**. It is most likely that this change was accidental, as is very often the case in **FE** (e.g. in the *Impromptu in A♭* Op. 29; cf. also commentary to the *Etude in C* Op. 10 No. 1, bar 1).

Bar 14 L.H. The prolongation of the third crotchet is indicated in **GE** only.
R.H. Added arbitrarily before the final note in **EE** is ×. *See* note to bar 68.

Bar 26 L.H. On the second crotchet, **GE** has only the upper note, *e¹* (probably an oversight).

Bars 28-29 L.H. The slurring given in the footnote is from **GE**.

p. 19

Bar 30 L.H. In the last chord, **FE1** (→**FE2**) has *g♯¹* instead of *e♯¹*. Chopin corrected this error in **FESch** and **FES**. The correct text is also printed in **FE3**, **EE** and **GE**.

Bars 31, 35, 102 and 106 Instead of semiquaver pauses **GE** has dots extending the value of the first chord, and the slurs over these phrases are not broken. **AI** has a similar rhythmic notation.

Bars 32, 36, 103 and 107 L.H. As the top note of the first chord **GE** has *a♯¹* in bars 32 and 103 and *a♯* in bar 36 (in bar 107 **GE** has *b*, as in the remaining sources). Given that this version is also found in **AI**, it is undoubtedly an original version, and was probably changed by Chopin in the manuscript bases for **FE** (→**EE**). Those later collected editions that give the version with *a♯¹* and *a♯* also arbitrarily altered *a♯* to *b* in bar 107.
R.H. Missing before the fifth quaver in **FE1** (→**FE2**) is ♯. In **FES**, Chopin added the signs in bars 103 and 107. **FE3**, **EE** and **GE** have the correct text.

Bars 37-38 and 108-109 The main text is taken from **FE** (→**EE**), the variant from **GE**. **AI** preserves the original form of these bars:

bars 37-38

bars 108-109

Chopin would have subsequently improved these bars in various ways in the manuscript bases for **FE** and **GE**, although given the present state of sources it is not possible to determine whether he considered one of the printed versions as definitive.

Bar 39 The *sostenuto* comes from **FE** (→**EE**), and *pp* was written by Chopin in **FED**. In **GE**, the D major section begins *f*, yet probably already in the basis for **FE** Chopin changed the dynamic conception (see note to bars 47 and 51), which is confirmed by *pp*, added later in **FED**.
L.H. As a grace note **GE** erroneously has *C#₁*.

Bars 39-46 **GE** does not have the slurs in the L.H. part.

Bar 41 R.H. On the fourth crotchet of the bar, only **FE** (→**EE**) has *a¹*. See *Performance Commentary* to bars 41, 49 and 53.

Bar 45 R.H. On the fourth crotchet of the bar the ♯ raising *g* to *g#* was undoubtedly omitted inadvertently by Chopin. It was not added until **GE**2 (after the composer's death).

Bar 46 R.H. In **GE** the minim *b¹* is tied to *b¹* on the fourth crotchet of the bar. This tie was probably removed by Chopin while proofreading **FE** (→**EE**). The repetition of *b¹* seems more natural: it corresponds to the repetition of *e¹* in bar 45 and fits the *crescendo*.

Bar 47 and 51 In **GE** *ff* occurs already in bar 47, while in **EE** it is missing altogether.

Bar 48 The sign ⟨ in this bar appears in **FE** (→**EE**). It may be argued whether it was not erroneously added by the engraver of **FE**, confused by the graphical similarities between bars 48 and 49.

Bar 49 R.H. In the second half of the bar, only **GE** has the tie sustaining *a¹*. See *Performance Commentary* to bars 41, 49 and 53.

Bar 50 L.H. In **GE**, the sixth octave is the same as the fourth and eighth, i.e. *A₁-A*. This is possibly an error.

p. 20
Bar 53 R.H. The main text comes from **FE** (→**EE**), the version given in the footnote from **GE**. See *Performance Commentary* to bars 41, 49 and 53.

Bars 53-57 L.H. **GE** has dots prolonging the quavers (as in the previous bars) instead of semiquaver rests.

Bar 58 R.H. The *b¹* in the chord at the beginning of the bar appears in **FE** (→**EE**), but not in **GE**. The version with *b¹* refers in sound to bar 56, whilst the version without *b¹* continues the arrangement of the previous bar.
L.H. In **GE** there is a slur over the whole bar.
L.H. Vertical lines, most probably indicating the passing of the fourth, sixth and eighth quavers to the R.H., are added in **FES** and **FED**. See *Performance Commentary*.

Bars 59-60 In **FE** (→**EE**) the moment of the return to the proper, initial tempo is not explicitly indicated (one can only infer it from the dashes limiting the extent of the *rall.* to the end of bar 58). **GE** has **in Tempo** at the beginning of bar 59. We follow **FE**Sch, where Chopin added a similar marking, but somewhat later.

Bar 61 and 73 **FE** (→**EE**) has only the sign 𝄢 at the beginning of these bars, which could be understood as a general indication *con pedale* (cf. *Etude in E♭* Op. 10 No. 11, bars 3, 11 and 34). The remaining pedal marks given by us Chopin added in **FES**.

p. 21
Bars 67-68 The pedal marks were added by Chopin in **FE**S.

Bar 68 **EE** has ♯ before the fifth note in the L.H. and the final note in the R.H. These markings were undoubtedly added by the reviser of this edition, guided by a conventional sense of harmony. Cf. note to bar 14.

Bar 72 R.H. The main text is reproduced from **FE** (→**EE**), the variant from **GE**. **AI** has a different rhythm to the melody throughout the bar: [musical notation].

Bar 74 R.H. Chopin wavered and changed the version of the last crochet of this bar several times:
— **AI** initially had a version with the triplet *e#²-d#²-b¹*, in which Chopin subsequently changed the last note from *b¹* to *c#²*;
— in **GE**, Chopin returned to the original version;
— **FE**1 (→**EE**) has a version similar to bar 20 (*d#²-b¹* quavers);
— in **FE**2 (→**FE**3), Chopin added the grace note *e#²*.
In the main text, we give the latest version, i.e. **FE**2, while the musically equiponderant original version, accepted for print by Chopin in **GE**, is given as a variant.

Bars 75-81 R.H. The additional crotchet stems appearing in bars 75, 78-79 and 81, as well as the head and stem of the minim in bar 76, appear solely in **GE**.

Bars 77-81 Some of the pedal marks appearing in **FE** (→**EE**) and **GE**) are complementary, whilst others can be deemed alternatives for one another. We give them all, as the markings in particular sources are incomplete and inconsistent.

Bar 80 R.H. In **GE**1 the second triplet sounds *a#¹-d#²-f#²*. This is the original version (appearing in **AI**), changed by Chopin to *a#¹-b¹-d#²* most probably in the manuscript basis for **FE** (→**EE**). This altered version was also employed in **GE**2.

p. 22
Bar 82 L.H. The accent above *c#¹* was added by Chopin in **FE**D.

Bars 82-93 Apart from the *leggiero*, which appears in all the original editions, **GE** has no other dynamic markings in these bars. They were most probably added by Chopin in the final stage of preparing the base text for **FE**. Cf. *Performance Commentary*.

Bars 82-100 R.H. In **GE** these bars are covered by a single slur.

Bars 83 and 89 R.H. The version given in the variant comes from **AI** and **FE** (→**EE**). This is most probably the original version, changed by Chopin in the basis for **GE**. The chromatic progression in this latter version (our main text) is more in keeping with the remaining part of the scale figuration of these bars than the broken thirds of the original version. The ascending four-note progressions on the fourth crotchets of bars 82-85 and 88-91 echo the four-note figures leading up to the highest notes in the middle of these bars.

Bars 84 and 91 L.H. The main text comes from **FE** (→**EE**), the variants from **GE**.

p. 23
Bar 87 L.H. As the fourth quaver **GE** has the chord *f#-g#-d¹*. A comparison with **AI**, in which this chord appears both here and in bar 93, proves that this is the original version, doubtless left by Chopin inadvertently. In removing *d¹*, Chopin wished probably to avoid the clash with *d#²* in the R.H.

p. 24
Bar 92 R.H. In **FES**, written above the first note of each of the four groups of demisemiquavers in the second half of the bar is the fingering 4. Given that Chopin's fingering in the similar figuration in bar 86 results naturally from the order of black and white keys, it would seem that the figures in bar 92 were written in by error (they may possibly have been intended for the second note in each group).

Bars 92-93 R.H. The last five demisemiquavers of bar 92 and the first two of bar 93 are given in the version introduced by Chopin in the proofreading of **FE**2 (→**FE**3) and – most probably – in the base copy for **EE**1. In the remaining sources (including **EE**2) these bars repeat the shape of analogous bars 86-87.

Bar 93 L.H. As the first note, **FE**1 (→**FE**2) has *a#*. This error was corrected in **FE**3.

Bars 94 and 96 L.H. The ties sustaining *g#* and *g#¹* are reproduced after **AI**. In **GE**, instead of the tie linking the two *g#¹* on the sixth and seventh quavers in bar 94, there is a motivic slur between *g#-c#¹*, whilst **FE** (→**EE**) has similar slurs in both bars. These versions are probably the result of an erroneous reproduction in the original editions of the notation of the autographs (with ties as in **AI**). The pairs of chords repeated in alternation, based on a similar harmonic scheme, can be found in the *Sonata in B♭ minor* Op. 35, movt. I, bars 81-85 and similar. Also there, the common note of the chords is repeated only in the second pair, based on the dominant and tonic of the principal key of a given fragment.

Bar 95 L.H. The first half of the bar evolved as follows:

AI

GE
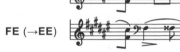

FE (→**EE**)

This last version, harmonically and rhythmically the smoothest, and most probably the latest, can be held to be the final one.
L.H. The note *a#* on the seventh quaver of the bar, together with the beam linking it to the *b* in the R.H., is found in **EE** only. This is probably one of the additions made by Chopin to the copy of **FE**1 which served as the basis for this edition.

Bars 95 and 97 R.H. As the first two notes, **AI**, **GE** and **FE**1 have *e³-f#³*. Chopin changed them to *a#²-e³* in the base copy for **EE** in bar 95, and in the proofs of **FE**2 in bar 97. We adopt these complementary modifications as expressing Chopin's latest intention.
R.H. As the third demisemiquaver of the fifth group **AI** and **GE** have *e¹*. We give the *e#¹* appearing in **FE** (→**EE**) as an undoubtedly later version.

Bar 96 L.H. **GE** has an additional *d#* on the second quaver and *d#¹* on the sixth quaver. In **AI**, *d#* and *d#¹* initially appeared in both bar 94 and 96; Chopin subsequently eliminated the striking of these notes in the repetitions of the motif: *d#¹* on the sixth quaver in bar 94 was removed, and *d#* on the second quaver of bar 96 was tied to the preceding note. In **FE**, this process was consistently carried through: *d#* appears only on the second quaver of bar 94, when this motif, introducing a new harmony, appears for the first time. It therefore appears highly probable that in the manuscript basis for **GE** Chopin partially copied the text of **AI**, forgetting to introduce the intended corrections.

Bar 97 L.H. In the first quaver, **AI** and **GE** additionally have *a#²*. Later corrections of the R.H. part (see note to bars 95 and 97) show that Chopin definitively abandoned this version.
R.H. As the third demisemiquaver of the seventh group, **AI** and **GE** have *g#¹*. We do not take account of this original version, altered by Chopin most probably in the manuscript basis for **FE**.

Bars 97-98 L.H. **AI** and **GE** have the following version:

We omit it here as it was most probably rejected by Chopin.

p. 25 *Bars 98-100* In **GE** *dim.* does not appear until the second quaver of bar 100.

Bar 100 𝆏𝆏𝆏 was added by Chopin in **FE**D.

Bar 101 R.H. In **FE** (→**EE**) the first note has the value of a crotchet. **AI** also has a crotchet here, yet marked *staccato*. The quaver appearing in **GE** is undoubtedly Chopin's improvement of the notation, as is confirmed by a clear sign of phrase division written here by the composer in **FE**D.
L.H. In the penultimate chord, **FE**1 (→**FE**2,**EE**1) has *f#¹* instead of *g#¹*. Chopin corrected this error in **FE**Sch and **FE**S. The relevant correction was also made in **FE**3 and **EE**2.

Impromptu in G flat major, Op. 51

Sources
A   Autograph fair copy intended as a basis for the original German edition (Library of Congress, Washington). **A** displays quite numerous inaccuracies in the notation of accidentals.
GE1 Original German edition, F. Hofmeister (2900), Leipzig, April 1843, based on **A**. **GE**1 was proofread by Chopin, and also bears traces of editorial alterations.
GE2 Second impression of **GE**1, in which several errors are amended.
GE = **GE**1 and **GE**2.
FE   Original French edition, M. Schlésinger (M.S. 3847), Paris, May 1843. **FE** is based on a proof of **GE**1 and was corrected by Chopin. It contains a substantial amount of errors. There are copies with the wrong order of pages (cf. quotations *about the Impromptus...* before the musical text).
FED, **FE**S, **FE**J – pupils' copies of **FE** with annotations by Chopin containing a few corrections of printing errors, fingering and performance indications:
   FED – copy from the collection belonging to Chopin's pupil Camille Dubois (Bibliothèque Nationale, Paris);
   FES – copy from the collection belonging to Chopin's pupil Jane Stirling (Bibliothèque Nationale, Paris);
   FEJ – copy from the collection belonging to Chopin's sister Ludwika Jędrzejewiczowa (Fryderyk Chopin Museum, Warsaw).
EE   Original English edition, Wessel & Stapleton (W & S. 5304), London, April 1843, based on **FE** or a proof thereof. **EE** bears evidence of editorial alterations and was not corrected by Chopin.

Editorial principles
Adopted as the basic source is **A**, with account taken of Chopin's later changes in **GE** and **FE**. We also take into consideration the additions in the pupils' copies.

The title and tempo indication
In his correspondence with publishers, Chopin called this work an *Impromptu* both prior and subsequent to its publication (cf. quotations *about the Impromptus...* before the musical text). Such a title is also borne by **A**, as well as by **FE** (→**EE**), which Chopin proofread. **GE** gives the title **Allegro vivace**, which undoubtedly arose from a misunderstanding: Chopin wished to use this term to replace not the title but the original indication **Tempo giusto** appearing in **A** (→**GE**). Eventually, in correcting **FE** (→**EE**), Chopin defined the tempo of the *Impromptu* as **Vivace**.

p. 26 *Bar 3* R.H. The accents are added in **FE**S.

Bar 6 R.H. As the third quaver, **FE** (→**EE**) erroneously has *c♭²*, which Chopin corrected in **FE**D and **FE**S.
R.h. Before the last quaver the sources lack the ♭ restoring *a♭¹*. Chopin's oversight is testified by ♭ appearing in all the sources in the analogous bar 79.

Bar 10 R.H. As the final quaver of the first half of the bar **GE**1 (→**FE**→**EE**) has *g♭²*. Chopin corrected this error in **FE**J and **FE**S. The correct text also appears in **GE**2.

9

p. 27   *Bar 11* r.h. Before the ninth quaver the sources are lacking the ♭ restoring *ab*¹. Chopin's error is testified by ♭ appearing in all sources in the analogous bars 27 and 84.

Bar 13 R.H. The grace note *gb*¹ is found in **A** (→**GE**). In **FE** only its head was printed, which makes it practically impossible to discern its signification. This resulted in the lack of the grace note in **EE** and in some of the later collected editions.

Bars 14, 30 and 87 R.H. **FE** (→**EE**) does not have the ∿ above the second quaver. This is most probably due to the engraver of **FE** misreading the unusual mordent mark used in **GE**.

Bar 15 R.H. **A** (→**GE**) lacks the ♭ restoring *eb*¹ on the ninth quaver. This sign was added in the correction of **FE** (→**EE**).

Bar 16 R.H. **A** lacks the tie sustaining *bb*¹. This error was corrected in **GE** (→**FE**→**EE**).

Bar 17 R.H. Before the eleventh quaver the sources lack accidentals. The inadvertent omission of the ♮ before the upper note (*c*³) is beyond question. Also the lack of the ♭ restoring *eb*² in the lower voice is most probably an oversight by Chopin (cf. characterisation of **A** and notes to bars 6, 11, 15, 26 and 83, 48).

Bar 19 ⎯⎯ is found only in **A**. Its lack in **GE** (→**FE**→**EE**) may be due either to the engraver's oversight or to Chopin's correction.

p. 28   *Bar 21* **FE** (→**EE**) lacks the 𝆏𝆏 (most probably an oversight).

Bars 23-25 The dynamic marks given by us in parentheses were added by Chopin in **FE**S.

Bar 24 **GE** (→**FE**→**EE**) has ⎯⎯ here, as in the identical bar 23. It appears highly unlikely that this sign would have been added by Chopin, especially given the 𝆏𝆏 added later in **FE**S (cf. note to bars 23-25). Thus, it is probably an engraver's error or editorial alteration.

Bar 25 L.H. **A** (→**GE**→**FE**→**EE**) lacks the chromatic signs before the final chord. The ♮ raising *gb* to *g* was added by Chopin in **FE**S. However, doubts may also be raised concerning the pitch of the upper note of this chord (*e*¹ or *eb*¹), since the *e*¹ appearing earlier was written by Chopin on the upper staff. The imprecise notation of this chord indicates that Chopin considered it obvious. Given the almost identical harmonic progressions in bars 9 & 82, and also the fact that the note *e* which appears from bar 23 onwards is part of the chord on which the harmony of these bars is founded, the only chord to be considered obvious is *g-db*¹-*e*¹.
Therefore, the chords *g-db*¹-*eb*¹ or *gb-db*¹-*eb*¹ given by some later collected editions most probably fail to correspond to Chopin's intentions.

Bars 26 and 83 L.H. In **A**, Chopin inadvertently omitted both the ♮ raising *cb*¹ to *c*¹ and also the ♭ subsequently restoring *cb*¹. Both accidentals were added in the correction of **GE** (→**FE**→**EE**). Cf. bar 10.

p. 29   *Bars 31 and 88* **GE** (→**FE**→**EE**) unifies the rhythmic notation of the second half of the bar following bars 7 and 15. However, in **A** the different notation of the L.H. rest that ends these bars impels one to distinguish bars 7 and 15, in which it applies to the upper voice alone, from bar 31 (bar 88 is not written out in **A**), in which Chopin wrote it clearly lower, as applying to the whole L.H. part. So, the lack of dots prolonging the minims *db* and *cb*¹ in bars 31 and 88 cannot be deemed an oversight by Chopin. The shortening of these notes is justified by the linking with the following bar: in the L.H. via a leap in the bass from *db* to *Gb₁*, in the R.H. with the lack of a direct resolution of *cb*¹ to *bb*.

Bars 32-34, 37-38 and similar. R.H. **A** has the following slurring:

(in **A**, bars 84-100 are marked as a repetition of bars 27-43.)
In the original editions, these slurs were reproduced with minor alterations, most probably of an accidental nature. In bars 33, 37, 89 and 94, Chopin added in **FE**D slurs linking the last quaver of these bars with the preceding quavers, while in bars 32, 37, 89 and 91 he placed a line separating the same last quaver from the subsequent bar. Given that in **FE** the final quavers in bars 38, 90 and 95 are printed – due to the above-mentioned inaccuracies – as linked to the preceding notes, it is clear that in relation to **A**, **FE**D displays consistent changes of phrasing in nine out of the ten places, including six marked by Chopin in his own hand. In this situation, deeming the altered phrasing to represent Chopin's final conception, it is the only one reproduced in our edition.

Bar 33 The ⎯⎯▷ sign appears in **A**. **GE** (→**FE**→**EE**) erroneously has ◁⎯⎯ instead. Similar engraver's errors are also encountered in other works, e.g. the *Nocturne in Db* Op. 27 No. 2, bar 6, and the *Etude in C minor* Op. 10 No. 12, bar 53.

Bars 37-38 and 94-95 Ties sustaining *eb* and *eb*¹ are found in **A**. In **GE** (→**FE**→**EE**) the R.H. tie in bars 37-38 wrongly begins one note too early, i.e. on *eb*¹ in the middle of bar 37. Moreover, **FE** (→**EE**) lacks the L.H. tie in bars 37-38 and the R.H. tie in bars 94-95. We give the unquestionable version of **A**.

Bars 38 and 95 R.H. **A** has the sixth *gb*²-*eb*³ as the final quaver. Chopin corrected his error when proofreading **GE** (→**FE**→**EE**; as a result of an imprecise realisation of the correction **GE**1 has *gb*²-*eb*³-*gb*³ in bar 95).

Bar 44 R.H. The main text comes from **A**, the variant from **GE** (→**FE**→**EE**). Graphical and psychological evidence suggest a possible error both by Chopin in writing **A** and by the engraver of **GE** in reading this notation. The following arguments speak in favour of the **A** version:
— the extension of the top note of a motif through an anticipated, syncopated striking is one of Chopin's characteristic methods of varying a rhythmic succession; cf. e.g. *Ballade in G minor* Op. 23, bar 167 in relation to bar 166 and also 107 and 175, *Concerto in E minor* Op. 11, movt. II, bar 28 in relation to bar 27, and bar 85 in relation to bars 84 and 35-36;
— the version of the first editions can, with a large degree of probability, be attributed to engraver's error or to the editor's amendment of a supposed error by the composer.
In favour of the version given as a variant is the possibility of Chopin's error in **A**, subsequently corrected by himself in **GE** (→**FE**→**EE**). Cf. note to bar 101.

p. 30   *Bar 48* L.H. **A** lacks the ♮ before the eighth note (*c*). This clear oversight on Chopin's part was corrected in **GE** (→**FE**→**EE**).

Bar 49 **GE** (→**FE** →**EE**) has, unlike **A**, a 𝄴 time signature. The replacement of 𝄵 by 𝄴 is one of the most common arbitrary changes in the first editions of Chopin's works (cf. commentary to the *Impromptu in Ab* Op. 29, bar 1, and also, e.g. to the beginning of movt. I of the *Concerto in F minor* Op. 21).

Bars 49-69 L.H. In the dotted rhythm (♩. ♪), which appears fifteen times in these bars, **GE** always places the semiquaver after the third note of the corresponding triplet of the R.H., which is contrary to Chopin's understanding of this rhythmic figure (cf. *Performance Commentary*). The engraver of **FE** (→**EE**), possibly better acquainted with Chopin's idiosyncratic notation, restored the proper alignment of the notes.

N.B. Corrections in bars 49-50 that are visible in **A** show that Chopin began to write this section in the 12/8 time which had been in force from the beginning of the work:

Only when reaching the four-quaver groups in bar 51 did he deem the notation in ¢ time, with triplets in the R.H., more natural and comfortable, identifying $\frac{12}{8}$ ♪♪♪ with ¢ ♪♪♪. (See *Appendix VIII* in: Jan Ekier, *Introduction to the National Edition. Editorial Problems*; available on www.pwm.com.pl.)

p. 31

Bar 62 R.H. As the final stroke of the first triplet, **GE** (→**FE**→**EE**) has *bb¹* only. This seems unlikely to be a correction by Chopin, since in **GE** there are no traces here of any changes being made.

Bar 65 R.H. On the ninth quaver of the bar **A** has the triad *ab¹-cb²-eb²*. Chopin removed the *cb²* in proofreading **GE** (→**FE**→**EE**). Cf. bar 53.

Bar 71 L.H. As the third crochet **FE** (→**EE**) has *eb* instead of *gb*. This error also appeared initially in **GE**, where it was corrected in the final phase of proofreading. Chopin restored the *gb* in all three pupils' copies.

Bar 74 L.H. The dynamic mark in the second half of the bar was added by Chopin in **FE**S. It may indicate either diminuendo or a long accent under the triplet on the third crotchet of the bar.

Bars 74-75 The *ritenuto* was added by Chopin in proofreading **GE** (→**FE** →**EE**).

p. 32

Bar 78 L.H. **A** (→**GE**) has *bb* instead of *gb* on the ninth quaver of the bar. Chopin corrected his error in proofreading **FE** (→**EE**). Cf. bars 5, 13, 29 and 86.

Bar 79 L.H. As the seventh quaver **GE** (→**FE**→**EE**) erroneously has *ab*.

Bar 84 R.H. The main text comes from **GE** (→**FE**→**EE**), the variant from **A**. Chopin probably added *ab¹* on the second quaver in proofreading **GE**, wishing to somewhat embellish and differentiate the final recapitulation of the theme. The version of the original editions may, however, also be the result of error on the part of the engraver of **GE**, who began the progression in thirds one note too early.

p. 33

Bar 101 R.H. In the main text, we give the rhythmic notation of **A**, since it is highly probable that Chopin imagined the whole of the second half of the bar in a fourfold division. In the variant, we put forward the version of **GE** (→**FE**→**EE**), thus taking into consideration the possibility of an error by Chopin in **A** and its possible correction in **GE**. Cf. note to bar 44.

Bars 102-103 R.H. The slur beginning in the second half of bar 102 was added – most probably by Chopin – in the proofs of **GE** (→**FE**→**EE**).

Bar 104 R.H. The grace note *gb¹*, which appears in **A** at the end of the bar, is omitted in **GE** (→**FE**→**EE**).

Jan Ekier
Paweł Kamiński

11

WYDANIE NARODOWE DZIEŁ FRYDERYKA CHOPINA

Plan edycji

Seria A. UTWORY WYDANE ZA ŻYCIA CHOPINA

Seria B. UTWORY WYDANE POŚMIERTNIE

(Tytuły w nawiasach kwadratowych [] są tytułami zrekonstruowanymi przez WN, tytuły w nawiasach prostych // są dotychczas używanymi, z pewnością lub dużym prawdopodobieństwem, nieautentycznymi tytułami)

1 **A I**   **Ballady** op. 23, 38, 47, 52

2 **A II**   **Etiudy** op. 10, 25, Trzy Etiudy (Méthode des Méthodes)

3 **A III**   **Impromptus** op. 29, 36, 51

4 **A IV**   **Mazurki (A)** op. 6, 7, 17, 24, 30, 33, 41, Mazurek a (Gaillard), Mazurek a (z albumu La France Musicale /Notre Temps/), op. 50, 56, 59, 63

25 **B I**   **Mazurki (B)** B, G, a, C, F, G, B, As, C, a, g, f

5 **A V**   **Nokturny** op. 9, 15, 27, 32, 37, 48, 55, 62

6 **A VI**   **Polonezy (A)** op. 26, 40, 44, 53, 61

26 **B II**   **Polonezy (B)** B, g, As, gis, d, f, b, B, Ges

7 **A VII**   **Preludia** op. 28, 45

8 **A VIII**   **Ronda** op. 1, 5, 16

9 **A IX**   **Scherza** op. 20, 31, 39, 54

10 **A X**   **Sonaty** op. 35, 58

11 **A XI**   **Walce (A)** op. 18, 34, 42, 64

27 **B III**   **Walce (B)** E, h, Des, As, e, Ges, As, f, a

12 **A XII**   **Dzieła różne (A)** Variations brillantes op. 12, Bolero, Tarantela, Allegro de concert, Fantazja op. 49, Berceuse, Barkarola; *suplement* – Wariacja VI z „Hexameronu"

28 **B IV**   **Dzieła różne (B)** Wariacje E, Sonata c (op. 4)

29 **B V**   **Różne utwory** Marsz żałobny c, [Warianty] /Souvenir de Paganini/, Nokturn e, Ecossaises D, G, Des, Kontredans, [Allegretto], Lento con gran espressione /Nokturn cis/, Cantabile B, Presto con leggierezza /Preludium As/, Impromptu cis /Fantaisie-Impromptu/, „Wiosna" (wersja na fortepian), Sostenuto /Walc Es/, Moderato /Kartka z albumu/, Galop Marquis, Nokturn c

13 **A XIIIa**   **Koncert e-moll** op. 11 na fortepian i orkiestrę (wersja na jeden fortepian)

30 **B VIa**   **Koncert e-moll** op. 11 na fortepian i orkiestrę (wersja z drugim fortepianem)

14 **A XIIIb**   **Koncert f-moll** op. 21 na fortepian i orkiestrę (wersja na jeden fortepian)

31 **B VIb**   **Koncert f-moll** op. 21 na fortepian i orkiestrę (wersja z drugim fortepianem)

15 **A XIVa**   **Utwory koncertowe** na fortepian i orkiestrę op. 2, 13, 14 (wersja na jeden fortepian)

32 **B VII**   **Utwory koncertowe** na fortepian i orkiestrę op. 2, 13, 14, 22 (wersja z drugim fortepianem)

16 **A XIVb**   **Polonez Es-dur** op. 22 na fortepian i orkiestrę (wersja na jeden fortepian)

17 **A XVa**   **Wariacje na temat z** *Don Giovanniego* **Mozarta** op. 2. Partytura

18 **A XVb**   **Koncert e-moll** op. 11. Partytura (wersja historyczna)

33 **B VIIIa**   **Koncert e-moll** op. 11. Partytura (wersja koncertowa)

19 **A XVc**   **Fantazja na tematy polskie** op. 13. Partytura

20 **A XVd**   **Krakowiak** op. 14. Partytura

21 **A XVe**   **Koncert f-moll** op. 21. Partytura (wersja historyczna)

34 **B VIIIb**   **Koncert f-moll** op. 21. Partytura (wersja koncertowa)

22 **A XVf**   **Polonez Es-dur** op. 22. Partytura

23 **A XVI**   **Utwory na fortepian i wiolonczelę** Polonez op. 3, Grand Duo Concertant, Sonata op. 65

35 **B IX**   **Rondo C-dur** na dwa fortepiany; **Wariacje D-dur** na 4 ręce; *dodatek* – wersja robocza Ronda C-dur (na jeden fortepian)

24 **A XVII**   **Trio na fortepian, skrzypce i wiolonczelę** op. 8

36 **B X**   **Pieśni i piosnki**

37 **Suplement** Utwory częściowego autorstwa Chopina: Hexameron, Mazurki Fis, D, D, C, Wariacje na flet i fortepian; harmonizacje pieśni i tańców: „Mazurek Dąbrowskiego", „Boże, coś Polskę" (Largo), Bourrées G, A, Allegretto A-dur/a-moll

Okładka i opracowanie graficzne · Cover design and graphics: MARIA EKIER
Tłumaczenie angielskie · English translation: JOHN COMBER

Fundacja Wydania Narodowego Dzieł Fryderyka Chopina
ul. Okólnik 2, pok. 405, 00-368 Warszawa
www.chopin-nationaledition.com

Polskie Wydawnictwo Muzyczne SA
al. Krasińskiego 11a, 31-111 Kraków
www.pwm.com.pl

Wyd. II (zrewidowane). Printed in Poland 2023. Drukarnia REGIS Sp. z o.o.
ul. Napoleona 4, 05-230 Kobyłka

M-9013328-0-5
ISBN 83-920365-0-6